BRAIN GAME TREASURE HUNTS

JUNGLE PUZZLES

JUNGLE CITY

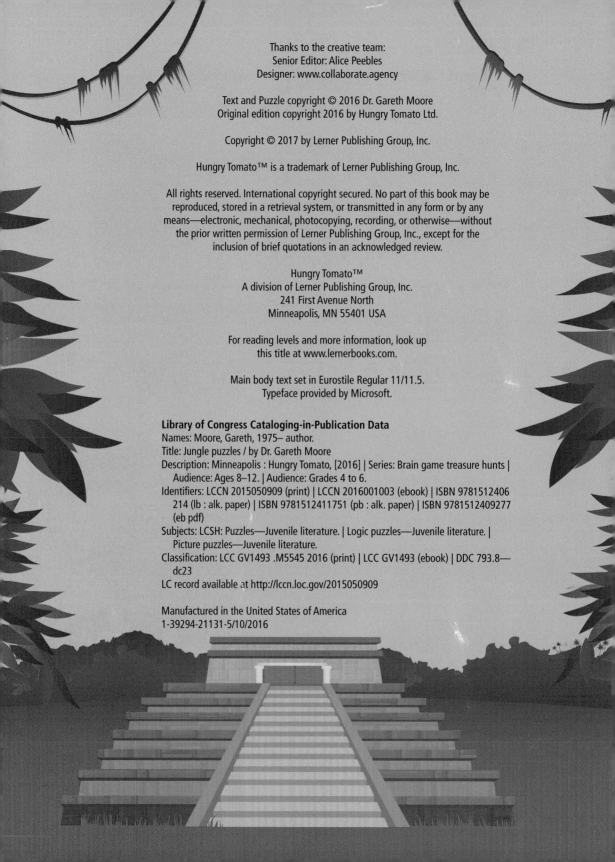

Thanks to the creative team:
Senior Editor: Alice Peebles
Designer: www.collaborate.agency

Hungry Tomato™
A division of Lerner Publishing Group, Inc.
241 First Avenue North
Minneapolis, MN 55401 USA

For reading levels and more information, look up
this title at www.lernerbooks.com.

Main body text set in Eurostile Regular 11/11.5.
Typeface provided by Microsoft.

Library of Congress Cataloging-in-Publication Data

Names: Moore, Gareth, 1975– author.
Title: Jungle puzzles / by Dr. Gareth Moore
Description: Minneapolis : Hungry Tomato, [2016] | Series: Brain game treasure hunts |
    Audience: Ages 8–12. | Audience: Grades 4 to 6.
Identifiers: LCCN 2015050909 (print) | LCCN 2016001003 (ebook) | ISBN 9781512406
    214 (lb : alk. paper) | ISBN 9781512411751 (pb : alk. paper) | ISBN 9781512409277
    (eb pdf)
Subjects: LCSH: Puzzles—Juvenile literature. | Logic puzzles—Juvenile literature. |
    Picture puzzles—Juvenile literature.
Classification: LCC GV1493 .M5545 2016 (print) | LCC GV1493 (ebook) | DDC 793.8—
    dc23
LC record available at http://lccn.loc.gov/2015050909

Manufactured in the United States of America
1-39294-21131-5/10/2016

BRAIN GAME TREASURE HUNTS

JUNGLE PUZZLES

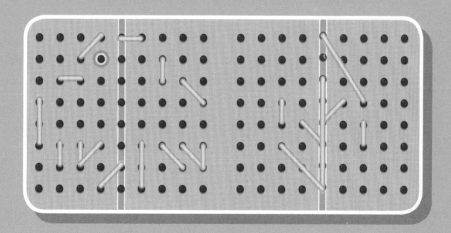

by Dr. Gareth Moore

HUNGRY TOMATO™

Minneapolis

CONTENTS

JUNGLE PUZZLES INTRODUCTION

You're on a trek along the famous Inca Trail, heading to the lost city of Machu Picchu. You are climbing a steep mountain path in the thick of the jungle. Suddenly the path gives way, and you find yourself plummeting down through the undergrowth deep into a narrow valley, with just a hint of sunlight creeping through the branches above . . .

This is a special kind of book. It contains a story with lots of puzzles, but these aren't normal puzzles like you will have seen before. These puzzles don't tell you exactly what to do—they provide only a certain amount of information, and then it's up to you to work out what to do and how to solve them!

If you get stuck or aren't sure how to solve a puzzle, there are hints provided. The hints are an important part of each puzzle, and you will need them for at least a few of the puzzles. When reading the hints for a puzzle, read them one at a time and only read the later hints if you are still stuck. Working out what to do is part of the fun!

A HIDDEN TEMPLE

You have landed in a small clearing, but you have fallen so far that there is no way to climb back up. In front of you stands an old temple. It has a number of paths that lead away from where you are, so you start by exploring them all to see if any of them will take you back where you came from.

A TEMPLE MAZE

Follow the four paths that leave the temple. Do any of them travel off the bottom of the map, escaping from the temple area? Or do these paths not connect to the temple?

There doesn't seem to be any way to go, other than into the temple. Above the entrance hangs a large sign:

TEMPLE SIGN

You feel sure this must identify the name of this place although it is not immediately obvious what it says.

Can you read the sign? There is a way to work out what it says. Do any of the letters look at all familiar?

You make a note of the temple's name in your notebook. It might become useful at some point.

THE WAY IN

You step toward the large doors and try to open them, but they won't budge.

You discover that the doors must be opened by a cog mechanism that will lift the doors upward rather than swinging them in or out. This mechanism requires a crank handle. You dig around in the undergrowth and eventually find the handle.

WHICH COG TO USE?

There are eight possible cogs, labeled A to H. The crank handle is hollow and will fit over the top of only one of the cogs. Which one?

You push the handle onto the cog, and it snaps into place.

OPENING THE DOOR

Now you need to work out which way to turn the handle—you don't want to break the door mechanism and end up stuck here forever!

The mechanism looks like this, with the crank handle at the bottom-right of the picture:

Which way should you turn the crank to open the door? Should it be turned in a clockwise or counterclockwise direction?

Turning the crank in the correct direction raises the door, and you grab your bag and enter the temple.

A HALL OF MIRRORS

As you enter the temple, you find yourself in a large entrance hall. The wall at the end has three open doorways. Each opens into the same room, which is full of mirrors. A map on the wall shows the exact layout of the room and the mirrors it contains:

THE MIRROR MAZE

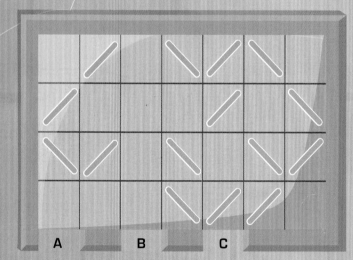

The doorways are labeled A, B, and C. Alongside the map is an example picture that explains something important about how light from a lamp will travel within this room:

Light will travel only horizontally and vertically between squares.
Notice how it shines out from the yellow lamp in the example.

Further text explains that there is only one grid square in the room where you can place a lamp so that the light from it can be seen at only **one** of the doorways: A, B, or C. The lamp must not be placed in the first square just inside a doorway, and the light from the lamp must not be reflected back onto the lamp itself.

In which of the thirteen squares that does not contain a mirror should you place the lamp?

THE THREE-FLOOR MAZE

Placing the lamp activates a hidden trapdoor that opens to reveal a maze. Within the maze there are more trapdoors that let you travel up and down between the three floors shown below.

Starting at the green circle, can you find your way to the exit, marked by the black arrow? Numbers show where the trapdoors that let you travel between floors are, but in every other way this works like a normal maze.

Starting from the green circle, explore the maze. When you reach a numbered trapdoor, you can climb through the trapdoor to another level by continuing from the same number on the floor above or below. Can you find a route all the way to the exit?

Eventually, by traveling between floors several times, you make your way safely out of the maze.

MANY HIDDEN MESSAGES

You exit the maze and find yourself in a small, dimly lit room.

As your eyes adjust to the gloom, you realize that the only source of light in this room is a strange, glowing orb located in the center of the ceiling. Perhaps it is lit from outside in some way?

On the wall in front of you are some curious, incomplete markings:

CURIOUS MARKINGS

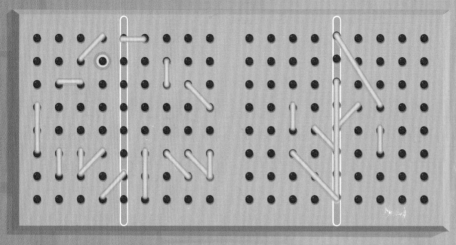

It's not clear what they are intended to represent, but what appears to be a list of options is written on the wall below:

TREE	**MOON**	**CANE**
BALL	**LEAF**	**TIME**
HILL	**DAWN**	**BIRD**
MAZE	**ROAD**	**SAND**

What do you think the markings mean? Which of the words on the list do they represent? Can you work it out?

After some thought, you decide on the words that the markings refer to and touch their places on the wall. With a loud rumble, the words crumble away and reveal a new puzzle:

SECRET MESSAGE

	2 1		1 2		2 1		1 2
2 1	**A**	1 2	**B**	1 2	**C**	2 1	**D**
	0 1		1 0		0 1		1 0
1 0	**E**	1 0	**F**	0 1	**G**	0 1	**H**
	2 0		0 2		1 1		1 1
1 1	**I**	1 1	**J**	0 2	**K**	2 0	**L**
	1 1		2 2		0 0		
1 1	**M**	2 2	**N**	0 0	**O**		

There is a hidden message in the red and hollow tiles above the letters and numbers panel, but can you work out how to read it?

Once you've discovered how to make sense of the tiles, speak the phrase you have just worked out. A path out of the room will be revealed.

STUCK IN A CHAMBER

You follow the path into another chamber.
The wall behind you slides back into place.

MYSTERY MATH FRIEZE

This room is decorated with various friezes recording different historical stories.
Your eye is drawn to one particular frieze that consists of columns of numbers and
mathematical operations. Some of the values are missing and have been replaced
by small spaces that contain question marks.

Lying on the floor are several tiles, each with a different number written
on it. They are shaped so that they will fit into the spaces in the frieze.

Which tile should fit into each of the question mark spaces?
Can you complete all three columns of the frieze?

A TILING PROBLEM

You work out what the numbers should be and place the correct tiles into their spaces. But nothing happens—perhaps there is more to do?

You look around and find another frieze. This time it is on the floor, with some empty sunken areas:

Below are four rectangular tiles. Each tile looks like it will fit into the right-hand side of one of the patterns on the frieze. The tiles look like this:

Now you just need to work out which tile goes in which sunken area!

Can you make sense of this second frieze? What do the patterns represent, and which of the empty sunken areas should each of the tiles fit into?

Slotting the tiles into the correct positions opens a panel in the ceiling, and a rope ladder drops down. You grab the ladder and climb up into the room above.

A DANGEROUS RIVER CROSSING

You climb up into a brightly lit room at the edge of the temple. Only a fast-flowing river prevents you from exiting the temple into the area beyond.

A series of stepping stones is laid out in the river, encouraging you to cross, but when you tentatively step on one, it crumbles away, and you nearly fall in!

You notice that each stepping stone is engraved with a letter, and colorful banners surround the stream.

STEPPING-STONE CHALLENGE

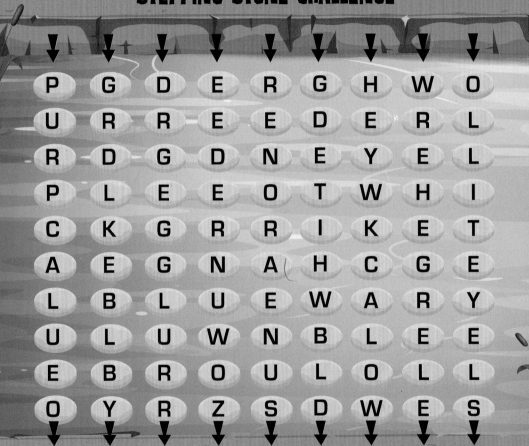

Start on any one of the stepping stones next to the top river bank and find a route across to the lower bank by moving only left, right, up, or down to neighboring stones—not diagonally. As you travel, you must spell out a series of RELATED words. Every brick you visit must form part of a word, and you can only form complete words—partial words are not allowed.

For example, from the stone at the top of the third column, travel right, down, and down to spell DEED, then right, down, and right to spell NOT—but these are not related words, so this is not the route. Can you make it to the other side?

Once across, you see five different trails of footprints that run in various directions. You suspect that the most recent of these will show you the way to go.

A

B

C

D

E

FOLLOW THE PRINTS

Can you work out which is the most recent set of footprints? Do they lead to point A, B, C, D, or E?

You identify the correct set of footprints and follow them.

THE KEY TO THE INCA ALTAR

The trail of footprints leads you into a clearing in the jungle. In the center there is a raised platform in the shape of an altar. On top of the altar there is a large, rusty chest. The chest is locked shut by two chains, which can only be opened by solving two puzzles.

UNLOCKING THE FIRST CHAIN

The first mechanism consists of three 2×2 panels, each consisting of four strangely patterned tiles:

Next to the panels a message has been inscribed:

REARRANGE EACH PART OF ME TO FIND THE KEY

What does this mean? The tiles can be taken out and swapped around within each panel, so could this be helpful? Although they can be moved, they can't be rotated. Using your imagination, can you work out what letter you could make by rearranging each panel appropriately?

You work out the key word, and the first chain releases!

UNLOCKING THE SECOND CHAIN

The second mechanism has similar panels, but these panels are blank, and there are twelve unattached tiles beside the chest:

Next to the tiles, another message has been written:

**FROM LEFT TO RIGHT,
I INCREASE IN HEIGHT.
MY RESULT IS SOMETHING OF
VALUE.**

Can you assemble each of the three panels correctly, using all of the loose tiles? None of the tiles need to be rotated. What is the "something of value" that results?

With the tiles in the correct positions, the second chain releases. Now you can open the chest! Perhaps a legendary treasure lies inside?

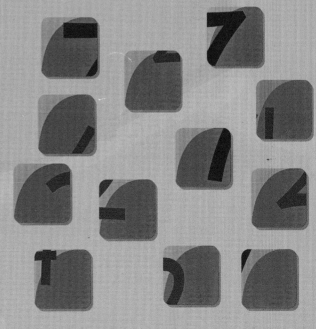

NEED THE SOLUTION? Turn to page 31.

A SECRET CHEST

You pull off the chains, open the lid, and are surprised to find a second, smaller chest hidden inside.

The lid of this smaller chest features an elaborate inlaid pattern, beneath which are six rotating letter dials. You can spin these dials to spell out any six-letter word you wish, and you soon realize that to open the box you'll have to work out what that six-letter word should be! The lid looks like this:

CHEST LID

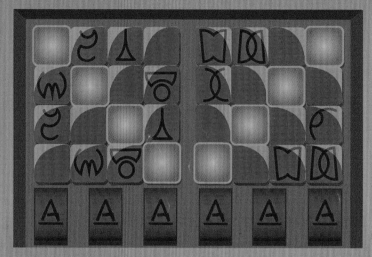

There is also a message written on parchment:

EACH EMPTY SQUARE REQUIRES A SYMBOL, BUT ONLY FOUR CAN BE USED PER GRID.

EACH ROW AND COLUMN HAS no REPEATS.

Inscribed on the lid of the chest is a letter-to-symbol key:

A C E I M N T y

By solving the puzzles and decoding the symbols, can you work out what the six-letter word is? This puzzle is tricky and consists of multiple steps, so if you get stuck, don't be afraid to use the hints!

HIDDEN PANEL COUNT

You dial in the correct word, and the lid of the smaller chest flips up,
revealing a second puzzle panel. This second puzzle looks like this:

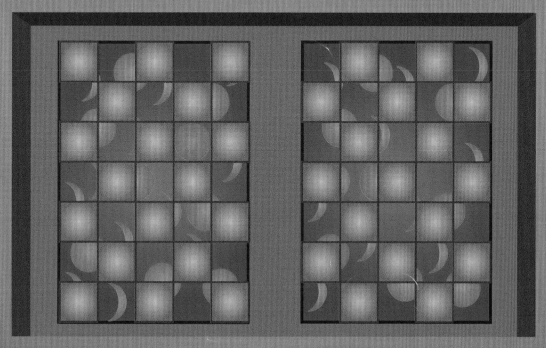

This panel has four more rotating dials, but these let you
enter digits from 0 to 9 instead:

You must work out the correct digits to set these dials to—but what should they be?

**Can you make sense of this second challenge? What do you think the sun and moon
symbols are for? And why are there two separate two-digit numbers to enter?**

After solving the puzzle, you set the four dials to
the appropriate values and are rewarded by the
second chest springing open!

A TILING PROBLEM

Inside the chest you find a rusty iron key, which fits snugly into a keyhole that you find on the side of the Inca altar. Turning the key makes the top stone of the altar turn over, revealing another surface.

PAIRING PROBLEM

The newly revealed altar top is ornately decorated, and in the very center is a set of sixteen illustrated tiles:

Experimentation reveals that each tile can be pressed like a button. You press one, and it stays down, but when you press a second tile, both tiles pop back up again. It seems that you need to find the correct two tiles to press down.

Which two tiles should you press? You are looking for two tiles that form a pair in some way. If you get stuck, don't forget to use the hints.

Pressing down on the two correct tiles causes the altar's supporting stones to collapse outward, revealing a deep chamber beneath.

WEIGHTS AND MOTION

Inside the chamber, there is a wall with three balances built out of woven vines hanging from small pulleys. Each balance has a fixed weight already placed on one side.

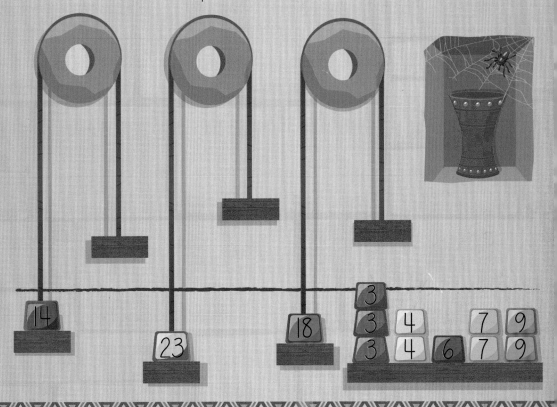

Next to the balances are ten smaller weights that can be moved onto the empty hanging platforms. You realize that you must move these smaller weights so that all three balances have an equal total weight on each side. Once this is done, all six platforms will be level with the line.

Which weights should you place on each of the platforms to balance all three systems? You cannot use more than one weight of each value on any individual balance.

After you've made all of the balances hang level, an opening appears in the wall. It contains a small flute and a few pieces of parchment.

ADVENTURE'S END

The flute is a simple instrument, cleanly carved out of a stick of hollow bamboo. It is drawn on one of the pieces of parchment, with numbers:

THE FINAL CHALLENGE

You aren't sure what meaning the numbers have, but based on your experiences so far, you are sure they must be significant!

There are two more pieces of parchment. One contains numbers, letters, and circles that match the flute holes. The third and final parchment contains a series of lettered clues.

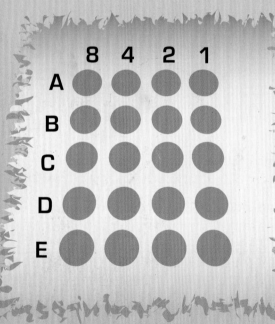

A. HOW MANY COLORS DID YOU NEED TO CROSS THE RIVER? SUBTRACT FROM THIS THE MIDDLE DIGIT OF THE SECOND CHAIN SOLUTION.

B. WHAT WAS THE NUMBER OF THE SECOND TRAPDOOR YOU USED IN THE THREE-FLOOR MAZE?

C. HOW MANY BALANCES CONTAINED BOTH A 4 AND A 7 WEIGHT?

D. WHAT IS HALF THE NUMBER THAT WAS MISSING FROM THE MIDDLE COLUMN OF THE MATHEMATICAL FRIEZE?

E. HOW MANY MIRRORS WERE THERE IN THE MIRROR MAZE?

PS THE ULTIMATE ANSWER IS 2.

Each letter clue results in a number. You must copy the flute chart and shade in some of the holes—but how? Don't forget that you'll know if you're correct because you'll find the "ultimate answer" of 2!

When you solve the puzzle, you reveal a sequence of notes to play on the flute.

You play the notes, which form a lullaby that
sends you quickly to sleep. When you wake up, you
mysteriously find yourself back on the Inca Trail.

Surely this whole adventure was just a dream? But
you check in your pocket and find a small, perfectly
carved flute . . .

JUNGLE PUZZLES HINTS

Not sure how to solve a puzzle? Use these hints to help.

Each puzzle has a series of numbered hints. Read hint 1 first, and see if it helps. Then only read each further hint if you still need it—at each step, the hints become more and more specific about how to solve the puzzle.

PAGES 6–7
A TEMPLE MAZE

1. Some paths cross over and under one another, but they don't join when they do this.
2. Try starting at one of the paths that leaves the area. Where does it go?

PAGES 6–7
TEMPLE SIGN

1. Does the second line look a bit like a regular four-letter word that you know?
2. The first letter of the second line is C. What has happened to a standard C to make it appear like this?
3. Each letter in the sign contains a second, overlapping and reflected copy of the same letter. Now you can decode it all.

PAGES 8–9
WHICH COG TO USE?

1. This is a mirror reflection of the cog.
2. The cogs may be rotated relative to the handle.
3. Eliminate cogs one by one. For example, B has one prong that is too small, so is not the match.

PAGES 8–9
OPENING THE DOOR

1. When a cog turns, all interlocking cogs turn in the opposite direction.
2. So which way does the cog that opens the door need to turn?
3. Work back along the chain of cogs, from the door to the crank handle. Not all cogs are important.

PAGES 10–11

THE MIRROR MAZE

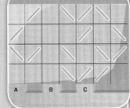

1. Eliminate squares that are right in front of a doorway, leaving eleven possible places to put the lamp.
2. Some of the squares can't light any of the doorways, so you can eliminate these as options.
3. Try pretending the lamp is outside entrance A, rather than in the room. Does it trace a path to any possible spaces where you could actually put the lamp?
4. Only the three remaining spaces directly above it could shine light to entrance B, so you could try each of these. Do all of them also light entrance C?
5. Try tracing a light path from entrance C. Of the squares it lights, are there any that fulfill all of the requirements for placing the lamp?

PAGES 10–11

THE THREE-FLOOR MAZE

1. The secret of solving this maze is being organized. Make a note of the trapdoor numbers you use, and then if you get lost, you can always retrace your steps and try another route.
2. Start by taking the passage that heads off to the left, not to the right. The first trapdoor to use is number 3.
3. The next trapdoor to use is number 9.
4. Not all trapdoors are used.

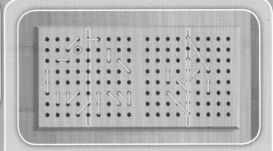

PAGES 12–13

CURIOUS MARKINGS

1. You've seen blue lines used as mirrors before, on page 10.
2. What would you see if you reflected one side of each image onto the other side, and vice versa?
3. Copy out the images, including the blue mirror line and all of the partial lines. Now, for each image, draw the reflection of the left half onto the right half, and the reflection of the right half onto the left half. What do you see for each image?

PAGESH 12–13

SECRET MESSAGE

1. You must convert the patterns in the upper panel into a two-word phrase—a 6-letter word and a 4-letter word.
2. There are two row-end numbers and two column-end numbers for each letter in the lower panel. How could these correspond with the upper panel?
3. Count the number of red squares in each row and column of the upper panel patterns. These correspond with the counts alongside the letters.
4. Use these counts to convert each pattern to a letter, revealing the two-word phrase.

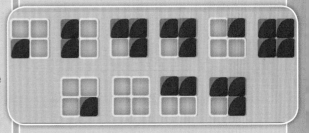

PAGES 14–15
MYSTERY MATH FRIEZE

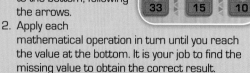

1. Start at the top of each column and work down to the bottom, following the arrows.
2. Apply each mathematical operation in turn until you reach the value at the bottom. It is your job to find the missing value to obtain the correct result.

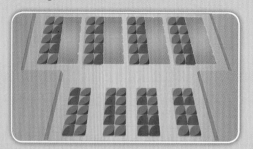

PAGES 14–15
A TILING PROBLEM

1. You don't need to rotate any of the tiles.
2. Draw out the possible options on some scrap paper if it helps. There are only four possibilities per area.
3. You are aiming to form a four-letter word.

PAGES 16–17
STEPPING-STONE CHALLENGE

1. "Colorful banners surround the stream" is a hint! Colors are the key to this puzzle.
2. The first step is onto the "P" in the first row, then to the "U" below. You now have "PU" so far.
3. Continue to "R," "P," "L," and "E," making PURPLE.
4. All the other words are also colors.
5. The next word starts with "G."

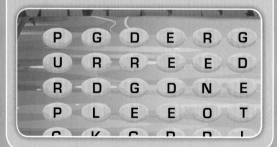

PAGES 16–17
FOLLOW THE PRINTS

1. You are looking for footprints that have left the temple the same way as you, so the set that emerges from the river is the right one.
2. This set is also on top of all the other prints in the trails, which means you can be certain it is the most recent and is the correct one to follow.
3. Trace the path carefully until you reach a letter.

PAGES 18–19
UNLOCKING THE FIRST CHAIN

1. Each panel can be rearranged to form a letter.

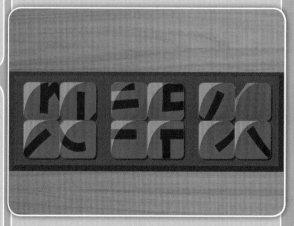

PAGES 18–19
UNLOCKING THE SECOND CHAIN

1. The pieces assemble to make a single digit in each panel. You need to imagine this process.
2. Pieces with digit fragments of the same color and line width fit together onto the same panel.
3. As per the message clue, the physically shortest number goes in the left-hand panel, and the tallest number goes in the right-hand panel. Each digit is drawn at a different height.

PAGES 20–21
CHEST LID

1. Copy out the grids rather than trying to solve this puzzle in your head.
2. Each grid solves like a sudoku puzzle without the boxed regions, placing one of each of the grid's symbols in every row and column.
3. You can translate the symbols to letters using the letter-to-symbol key.
4. After converting to letters, read along the two highlighted diagonals. These spell out a clue.
5. What is the solution to this clue? It is the same as the solution to the second puzzle in the book.

PAGES 20–21
HIDDEN PANEL COUNT

1. You are looking for a count of suns and moons.
2. The two images show the same picture, but you can see different parts on each side. You must combine them in your head to find the correct counts.
3. If you imagine copying all of the uncovered tiles in one image on top of the brown, covered tiles in the other image, how many suns and moons would you see? For a number less than 10, dial in 0 for the first digit.

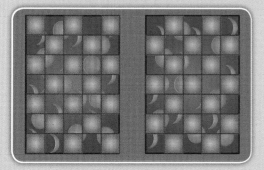

PAGES 22–23
PAIRING PROBLEM

1. None of the tiles are identical, but you need to look for a pair that have the same set of symbols.

PAGES 22–23
WEIGHTS AND MOTION

1. The loose weights come to the same total as the weights that are already placed. This means you must move all the weights to the right-hand side of the balances.
2. You must use all of the weights, with none left over.

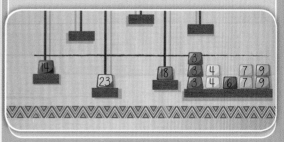

PAGES 24–25
THE FINAL CHALLENGE

1. Each of the lettered clues results in a number.
2. You can answer most of the clues using the Solutions section if you have forgotten the answers to previous puzzles.
3. How can you shade in the flute holes for each letter to match the number? The solution to A is 6, so what can you shade to represent 6?
4. Shade the "4" and "2" holes to represent 6.
5. Do the same with B, C, D, and E.
6. What does the pattern of holes look like? It should look like the digit 2.

JUNGLE PUZZLES SOLUTIONS

Most of the puzzles are explained in detail within the hints section, and only the end solution or any missing additional information is given here. To see how to reach each of the solutions given below, you should first read all of the hints for that puzzle.

PAGES 6–7
A TEMPLE MAZE
None of the paths lead away from the temple. Those that appear to do so do not actually connect to the temple:

PAGES 6–7
TEMPLE SIGN
Jungle City:

PAGES 8–9
WHICH COG TO USE?
Cog E

PAGES 8–9
OPENING THE DOOR
You must turn the crank handle counterclockwise. The chain of connected cogs and the way they turn will then be as shown here:

PAGES 10–11
THE MIRROR MAZE
The lamp should be placed as follows:

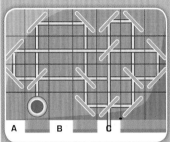

PAGES 10–11
THE THREE-FLOOR MAZE

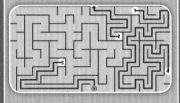

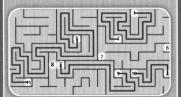

PAGES 12–13
CURIOUS MARKINGS
BIRD and LEAF:

PAGES 12–13
SECRET MESSAGE
HIDDEN GOLD

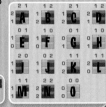

PAGES 14–15
MYSTERY MATH FRIEZE

14	10	12
×2	×3	÷2
−1	+10	×11
+15	÷8	−16
−9	×3	÷5
33	15	10

PAGES 14–15
A TILING PROBLEM

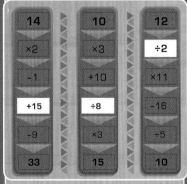

The word is OPEN.

30

PAGES 16–17
STEPPING-STONE CHALLENGE

Purple – green – orange – blue – brown – black – white – yellow

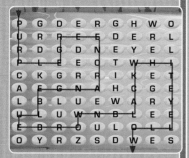

PAGES 16–17
FOLLOW THE PRINTS

B

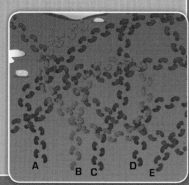

PAGES 18–19
UNLOCKING THE FIRST CHAIN

KEY

PAGES 18–19
UNLOCKING THE SECOND CHAIN

427

PAGES 20–21
CHEST LID

The completed grids look like this:

Reading along each highlighted diagonal from left to right, this spells out CITY NAME. The six-letter answer is therefore JUNGLE from the puzzle 2 solution, which told you that you were entering JUNGLE CITY.

PAGES 20–21
HIDDEN PANEL COUNT

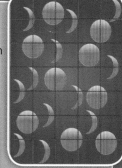

The combined image is shown by the picture to the right. This contains nine suns and twelve moons. The numbers to enter into the dials are therefore 09 and 12. If your answer was doubled by counting both grids, to give eighteen and twenty-four respectively, then that's also correct. Either solution is equally good, and both would open the lid of the chest.

PAGES 22–23
PAIRING PROBLEM

The matching pair is D2 and B4.

PAGES 22–23
WEIGHTS AND MOTION

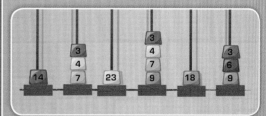

PAGES 24–25
THE FINAL CHALLENGE

A is 8 minus 2, giving a result of 6. B is 9. C is 2. D is half of 8, which is 4. E is 15.
Rewriting each of these results as a sum of 1, 2, 4, and 8, this gives A=4+2, B=8+1, C=2, D=4 and E=8+4+2+1.
Shading in the dots under those values to give these totals results in a flute tune parchment that looks like this:
The shaded (covered) holes look like the digit 2, thus fulfilling the "ultimate answer."
Phew! That was a complex puzzle! Very well done if you worked out all of that!

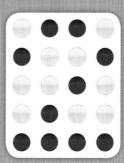

INDEX

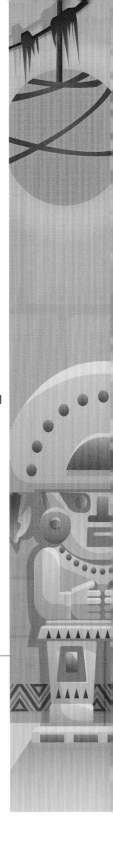

THE AUTHOR

Dr. Gareth Moore is the author of a wide range of puzzle and brain-training books for both children and adults, including *The Kids' Book of Puzzles, The Mammoth Book of Brain Games,* and *The Rough Guide Book of Brain Training.* He is also the founder of the daily brain-training website www.BrainedUp.com. He gained his PhD from Cambridge University (UK) in the field of computer speech recognition, teaching machines to understand spoken words.